A DOUBTFUL HOUSE

A Doubtful House

Alice B. Fogel

BAUHAN PUBLISHING
PETERBOROUGH NEW HAMPSHIRE
2017

Library of Congress Cataloging-in-Publication Data
Names: Fogel, Alice B., author.
Title: A Doubtful House : poems / Alice B. Fogel.
Description: Peterborough, New Hampshire : Bauhan Publishing, 2017.
Identifiers: LCCN 2016058355 (print) | LCCN 2017001134 (ebook) |
ISBN 978-0-87233-232-4 (softcover : acid-free paper) | ISBN 9780872332355 (eb-
ook) Classification: LCC PR9570.L43 H375 2017 (print) | LCC PR9570.L43 H375
2017 (ebook) | DDC 823/.92--dc23
LC record available at https://lccn.loc.gov/2016058355

To contact Alice, go to her website:
www.alicebfogel.com

Book design by Kirsty Anderson
Cover Design by Henry James
Cover painting: *Snakes and Ladders* by Julia Zanes, www.juliazanes.com
Photograph of the author by Mariah Edson

BAUHAN
PUBLISHING LLC
PO BOX 117 PETERBOROUGH NEW HAMPSHIRE 03458
603-567-4430
WWW.BAUHANPUBLISHING.COM
Follow us on Facebook and Twitter — @bauhanpub

MANUFACTURED IN THE UNITED STATES OF AMERICA

Contents

Phenomenal cosmic power!
Itty bitty living space.

—the Genie (Disney's *Aladdin*)

The Doubtful House

The house as far as the house can remember doesn't believe you
didn't always feel like this slogging
   through wet concrete a slippery foundation wonders were you your mood
                 then ephemeral unless captivated less a dense
humidity swells the interior pushes against un
even doors refuse to slam
     windows with dim views won't budge in any room here it's impossible
                to breathe so suggests you
stop trying not to wonder if everyone
who lives in a house with someone
                else is a little loony eventually
                 what was hard and fast
becomes hard and slow going without saying
uncomprehendingly laying
         blame the other for dampening everything being
               incomprehensible
where once you saw you were seen you were you and not you now you
suspect the very syntax
               of your thoughts
     have a life of their own don't they even if you don't or is it just you
who says everything you say
is strangely off like an unplumb house
       sinking into rotting sills east spun west on a compass
             like you're living bicoastally
or bipolarly freeze to your heat at the flip
to the other side
             of a wooden nickel
   mildewed inside out since when you can't recall can't understand how
to agree on the slightest thing the smallest
article of definite or indefinite

                                                              faith
                                      completely lost in this housemire
is like
walking into a wall the wall whatever
                              walls makes every hopeful house become a
                                                    doubtful house when
you could couldn't you evaporate unbeknownst take a second
home in some southern clime where it's clear and dry

House Keys

Other times you come home to the wrong house disbelieving the fit
of the keys in the locks deranged tantrum pushing
                                        open the door before you
                                        even have a chance
to wish it wouldn't against all reason go on
hanging your coat in the closet
                                        when it's late and you are coming from
                                        going to and arriving
at times you need to pause and get your bearings switch
on lights too bright to bear
                                        witness to whatever
                                        life this is or whose
skewed welcome mat whose leaning bats
in the belfry whose
                                        newel post grimy
            with so many hands unable to orient without that momentary
grasp the cool
slide of the gooseneck riser finding the moon
                                        windowed and radiant climbing
                                        like water forced
upward through subfloors by a talent for instinct in the dark
stairwell without knowing why
                                        you have returned what with all the lack
            of other options not yours not hours not the house's finest
combination of complaints canceling out into silences spinning
in you like houseflies in the overhead fixtures
                                        knocking to be let out
            or in to a room you don't question for one minute don't you
wish you were like the key
does exactly what it's meant to even if you won't

                                              stop burying it under the rug
                                    where you wipe mud off your shoes
even knowing everyone knows to look there even remembering
who first home waits upstairs in the bed can't help
                                    but be warm and pulls you like a magnet
                    draws conclusions to it under the quilts unlike yours seduces
in a language you don't have to speak
to be attached to its force
            of habit indistinguishable from love whether or not you are at home
                                    in it you might as well be
anywhere but here
is where you are built into this house lock and key

House of Answers

What you never learn   is that late in the night the house hosts flies
and bugs lightning and june biting   and stinging things calm

moths uncertain heart and dart   meet like guests on the painted walls
with their translucent greens   and pale glistening blue their blind

wings and thousand   actual eyes see more than you
ever will spread their metallic bodies   paper

the rooms with designs you would never   believe one night they spell
in ancient runes Sanskrit rules   another diagram in untranslatable

insect dialect all the positions   of the Kama Sutra
transform the house   into an aural sky

of constellations parallel male and female   universes read on cave walls
and closed lids   beam with meaning and you

asleep like drunken mystics dream   maps you never find routes you wish
you'd taken   care to follow reason

out of context   the broken patterns fresh starts you need you peal
with laughter and forgiveness you don't   remember in the morning

when you open   your mouths
and breathe in the dust fluttering from the walls and brush it from your eyes

House of Flight

The house knows it can fly but you weigh it   down like a grave with stones

believe only you can leave and then place   your sentimental souvenirs

of where else you've been in plain sight seeing tchotchkes on the endtables

tiny spines impossible feathers   from your escapes your exotic

vacations and flights   of fantasy to Paris

flea market chandeliers   affixed to the ceiling like manifested haloes

of unspoken thought   gifts brought back

not for the house or you but for proof   of belonging to the world

beyond a kitchen wall where you pin up   monthly baobabs and Himalayas

like blueprints   of alternate lives the house clearly sees

it's a convenience a shingled sided insulated box   of chocolates filled

with sugary blue light like ice in a glass or remote control the same weather

day in and day out   as if that kind of comfort

clinched the promise of to house and to hold   you should admit you want

so you can leave and leave   even when you stay

you leave   traces of your leaving home at home everywhere but

what if the world and the house were   more than you imagine you are

so obvious but where is   the house when you turn away

House of Talk

When you say what is
                              there to talk about the house suggests that is exactly
when you should start talking but is also
                                             aware that when you talk
you are like in the beginning
                                            was the word you are creating
what didn't yet exist what you don't even know
                               or think before you speak but the house
recommends you believe it anyway admit
                              what you don't say bleeds into what you do
like badly sorted laundry
                                          afraid of dying are you
before you've said everything
                                            or is this your death song
could you cut to the chase well could *you* cut it out
                               from the sutures of your lips or your brain's
immovable articulation find something
                                    anything to say did you even have
anything to say or are you just talking
                                                          listen

                       the house sighs wishes you'd switch roles
take a lingual pilgrimage track down what is
                              the holy grail of a conversation
or of two or at least one
                 and a half simultaneous monologues you don't know the other
half of it can't tell a thought
                   from a thought bubble the house observes as delicately

15

as possible that in verbal intercourse

                    you seem to have the same performance

anxiety and you

                          your rolling multiples

may be a cliché but not a case

                 of mistaken identities you still call

out the same names you called when you

                       married you why don't you

listen in the balance

                            you know who

and what you think

                               you hear

Thieves

Somewhere around a far corner like a thread
                                        following its needle through the dark

wing a cricket sings or maybe a door half unhinged
                                        swings the point being

not the end but because
                                        there is an end

unknotted slips through the house tonight so
                                        whatever thieves

touch turns theirs ends up their means
                                        what was never theirs seems to become

what was never there fingerprints the guilty
                                        pearls and knives shining in other hands in other

words the past the names and warranties of stuff
                                        kneeling in surrender in the distance between points

of entry and exist the addict and his fix between
                                        intention and wherewithal a house can take a hint hear a pin

falling for a song is this
                                        how it goes with things or without there goes

the deed
                                        done all in the bag the diamonds

the valuables along with everything else they take
                                        the variables down to negative

numbers the keys to what's material nine-tenths of
                                        the law

fully wedded holding dearly
                        on by a thread by such need how

can they take it
                        into their mortal hands oh

the empty O it must take
                                        so much

to want so much

House of Mirrors

Do you imagine the house   doesn't see you when undressed

you solicit mirrors memories of your better   form how are you different

from a teenager from the house each   with some vague yearning with

out knowing what for something lost   or not yet brought home

every house has a drawer   for things no one can find a room

you think you're invisible in this house   is a closet your whole life storage

flashing before your eyes   adjust to the inside

beyond frame the measurement   on centers the tongue and groove

of your lives passing   time

after time the house would like you to keep looking   till you see yourself

disappear or both   double takes in the house a backward glance

more mercurial than your   dread of regret as if you were alone

on that stage in your reflection you   find your skin shattering

close your eyes think   you are praying but all that is is hope

The Housing

The house ages just like you will notice dullness or flaking in the finish
gaps that weren't there before gaskets need replacing
holes filling so if you have to call in the specialists

when water pours down from the ceiling it's dangerous
to handle the wires cross the fault

is not the house's if settling or leveling happens
to be part of the deal you made in inverse
proportion to the benefits and pleasures of living

here a little weatherizing there some light repairs tears
in the tub don't mean it's all falling apart

from not being appreciated for more than beauty or strength
the steadfast roof or the impermeable plumbing depths for a way
with holding harboring no grudges staying

you might take notes from
the book of the house plan engage with what is

at hand conduct yourselves with warmth in winter be cool
under pressure patient with the long haul it takes
to be a house at all right with an inside understanding of rot and renovation

require a housing for those tender
enough to be chewed right through everything the house never thinks as "I"

but as conduit containment the coupling between you and you and the you
two become transformed into a new math the one
draining point of view

Charges

Because you are each what you feel and what you do
                                    because of or in spite of
that regret defines you as owned not owner
                                    of the house after all
is only a unit of measure a dwelling
                                upon degree of guilty habit
ation where you without a thought go
                                to be safe at home building
up a living pentimento like paint over wallpaper
                    year after year layering the invisible as space you see
as negative and the house could be a definition your temple
                athrob with private applause where however implausible you
complete each other's sentences
                                                or let them go
unserved weekend after weekend the house
                                waits and you dissembling deliberate
and legislate exchange vows like never again didn't mean to soon
                                retreat into the narrow nest
of what you feel and what you do
                    because of or in spite of that as if you are less
than a household a quorum
                                commissioned to buy and sell
an agreement made and kept not dropped and swept
                        into corners cut really who do you think you are
ever going to be houselings if you don't shape up to the blueprint
                                the fingerprints on the wall
know what you are
            in an arranged marriage hunted and brokered and mortgaged or rent
a part paid every month a value at the price a prize
                                open your eyes see the sign

21

on the roadside emergency

                        number of inhabitants who like you

stake a claim to who you can be

                        in possession of or repossessed

Footfalls

The house wishes it were a lotus
                                        or a nautilus whose stairwells
might leave themselves behind

                        calyx lightning strikes mud from the pond
slipped in on soles and sifted dry but floors oak and pine
                        alive through the night like violins after hours vibrate

the attic lets in nocturnals the closets clear their throats
                                would like to know what is the halflife
of five shoe boxes of incremental size piled inside

                        what opens blooms what unwinds what slides
through the clapboarded shell and over sills
                                flowers salt and ozone bow the air

tunes the balusters and rails
                        sheets of rain turns in sighs befall the roof
like footsteps little roots on risers morning dusk and noon

Guests

After three biblical days a little hardened glob   of marmalade under the lip
of the counter is just one of those things no one   will own up to
noticing a little piece of evidence   that things have changed though
you're not sure to what   was it that you walked out here for a gasp
of fresh air a little   rest perspective on the guests forget
which are guests whether or not they should   leave or feel at home
in your house they waft through the living room   like secondhand smoke
you breathe sun radiating from shingles   something burning in the distance
pleasantly   or threateningly it isn't clear
if walls had eyes they'd roll   in the same direction as water spiraling
down the drain clogged   with hair baby-fine Kool-Aid dyed or aging off
whose family   is this the most sane most complaining their cries
and laughter lofting out smudged windows   to the yard beget in you
opposing pleas to run toward   away
from all the questions clawing   through your closets and drawers
and mind   your manners which switch
goes with which light which always   is left on more juice more sweet
warm milk   with fingers on the rim more
cheesy kisses why   don't you ask them if they'd like to tear
through the contents of your heart   strings you along indefinitely not
that they weren't planning to   already without asking
who invited who   lives here you
turn back time   to go in now
move   in

24

The Closet

What else
                          do you think you can hide in there with your shapeless
uniforms your decades
                                                old clothes with overgrown
shoulder pads your ties wide as tanks sputtering out of oil
                                                fooling only fools
because when the language
                                        goes marching so does knowing
the birds native
          names left unuttered in their dusting feathers drop like deformed leaves
greasy on the closet floor hosting microscopic mites breed more
                                                mines in the walk in
territory of the raging mold
                                        you prowl like monster boars
at Chernobyl barely recognizable
                              strange and scary and changed your skeleton
keys hang around your neck clacking against a barrier of ribs barring
                              hearts whose importance in relation
to what kind of atmosphere permeates all the rest
                                                can hardly be
exaggerated but instead you think you can be unreactive closed up like one
                              cramped musty unbreatheable space
can't cover up the nuclear
                              meltdowns radiate through the entire house
the couch expanding to crush lamps and hassocks
                                        pushing away everyone
starving under
                  the dining table overgrown into another glass ceiling
the bureaus stained shut leaving no room for others
          belongings while you go on claiming you can store torn shirts

on spent rods and stuffing your boots scuffed with contaminated
                              dust the farmlands with toxic chemical
dependence upon industrial strength avoidance
                      of annoying bugs means you get no more free flights
of doves but three legged frogs
                                  raining like a plague of hangers
on toddlers with tumors in their cell phoned brains and so called
                      adults held hostage to microchips with missing
vocabulary for emoticons if you want to know the truth
                                  of who you are then open up
the door to that closet

The Constant House

Do you think you are more profound than the house
        because the house stays put on a poured foundation while you
shout and moan your reenactments
        and complaints of injustices are grand gesticulations the sole
indicators of depth and breadth what measures
                will you go to affirm what
in fact is your stasis however moving to yourself
            in comparison to the house for all you know
may be as constant as
        gripped by dread as spent on love is what the house is all about
shelter all about comfort all about you
        do not have a monopoly on utility or the electric shock
of either inarticulate sensitivity or articulate insensitivity you may have
        installed the lightning rod but who puts the roof over whose
head whose floor do you rest upon the house
            does not want to play
escape the room games or go to your room whenever you want out
           will not quake to validate
your coping techniques your kind
        of existence has no portal no safe room no fallout
bunker for rants and rages fill the house
        does what it does best stands
still
           for you

House of Bad News

When you fight do you hear what the house hears

                              inside the living

room for half a world away

                       with the fairies damages accrue

to you

                                don't see that

on the edge

                      of these woods and fields

are a window to a far and wide

                            screen world

of blackened blue

                                      air

you need

                          to breathe now

because when you turn on

                            each other

bad news

                            is natural

disasters unnatural

                      in every backyard

tornadoes kill six

              in Mississippi volcano ash darkens

all Europe and you are the less

                        able to escape

the knowledge of your limbic brain uncomprehending any tense

                difference between now and then

coping with the voices

            accumulate in urgent tones like accusations

that drone deploys

        while terrorists attack in Moscow and London and here

you are not listening because

how could the house

any more than human hearts

know in time

or space the distance

from that pulsing

piece of glass

to each day's number

of Shi'ites dead in Baghdad

mosques of Rwandans in your blood the century-old
Armenian genocide in your house now

the exact losses

of shoreline as the sea

swallows subcontinental islands

in your throat oil

swallows the sea

of forests collapsing in Paradise

you cannot fathom

when or how

the trees the ravaged the prayerful

dead explode

out of you when you argue

that is what the house hears and can't tell

apart from what is

about nothing

so much as whether

you define love at all

in the same universal

terms how could you

possibly not

know that

you do

Anniversaries

It starts with you
of yourselves afloat

carried away over the threshold shore
on an ether wave

forever more one paper date
in your eyes

to navigate by the stars
cotton to your love

of three leather armchairs armloads
the house like a boat shifts

of forget-me-nots but over time
angles untrue a new slant

to the wooden floors
things out again new wool

you every time sweets iron
over your eyes eventually see the light

of day and night you sail
through the eighth bronze age past

from year to year
the ageless age

of enlightenment formed from nine
you'll recall you

potsherds willed to the sun and moon
still are to you

illuminate who orbits who
who steals the center of the universe

tithes from the tin
in twelve silken tones laced

with bad luck
as well be from Mars

references to how sometimes you might
which doesn't necessarily mean that you are

Venus you know
ivory to save the fourteen elephants

you dovetail you spoon you skip
in the room side by side

you gaze at a crystal ball aglow with evening   news sitcoms reality shows
up less and less able to scale the twenty-league wall of China between you

and your silver lining years	and years rising daily charting
rough seas you hardly notice also hold	thirty pearls thirty-five coral reefs

teeming with life like the pirated chests as yet unburied blessings heartbeats
count now lift them while you still can	one by one

forty rubies forty-five sapphires before	they weigh too much cause
a gold rush from what might've been	for sixty years a bedrock of diamond

Playhouse

The house opens to a series of ruminations off a corridor
                                toward an idea shot in the dark
tavern to drink on the house a juxtaposition
                                of yours and mine the afterhours the house
thinking maybe
                                it is a playhouse
where actors and sideliners assemble
                                to take stock of tragedy comedy dramady and romance
feels like a tall order
                                high as the rooftops of heaven might be to script this thing
so circled divided and ruled
                                by what hemisphere
and what horizon a line onstage delivered in the voice
                                of the ascendant every morning
the descendants at dusk the lineage the house harbors
                                your aisled pacing in the shadows cast by houselights
stars lodged by the hearth so
                                come to bed lay your heads here
and here for house's sake
                                tomorrow you can pick through the sets
between partitions curtains and exits
                                play out your days splitting
hairs nights tearing up
                                ticket stubs

Summer House

All winter the house is an island

                                        housebound

kept on a shelf you hunch shut up

                                    and shivering covered

on couches and chairs

                                        separate bereft

you forget how it isn't to be so enclosed

                                    but never close

the distance

                        in tight spaces with the rug askew

to parallel rows in the flooring

                            could be the worst thing ever

for your sanity

                                            the most

unbreachable

                    sighs more stale airless strangers alone

and alone

                                                until

one morning the sun bends the corners illuminates the side yard you
            can't take your eyes off you again summer comes again
unruly mismatch blows the familiar inside
                            out go the barriers built or believed
of glass and coats place and self and time to urge open windows please
                        beat free from folds each house mite
sail the bedclothes over rails what does that feel like it feels like how the air
        blinks into fresh eyes how the ear hears the all along there now hold
ajar door after door up the street and down the county for the visitor sounds
                        of caws and calls forth neighborhood
negotiations stroke your shins with lawns
                soaped cars winded skin apple dust and here and there

are there and here you are
                in a lifting mist of dampness evaporating from under eaves mixed
with salt stewed seas Madagascar monsoons and Norwegian midnight suns
                                dry your eyes while the great equator
crosses latitudes to you with molecules
                                of Moroccan sand and Thai rice grains land
on your bare feet
                and the furred and feathered contents of the farthest continents
in this leaping lunging clime
                        all over each other to lap and overlap combustible
in spacious wilds sweep through you outwit both room and broom
                                the house now the world and you
and you
                        inclusive breathless breathing touched

The Kitchen

The house could be love or merely the container
that defines it like the sink

                                            defines the dishwater
                                 before it spirals down the drain
you could as you move to the stove shift for an opening
drawer the tines inside ticking

                                       in tandem like tangos
                 of thought turning again you step aside for a paring
knife the clove peeled and grating the chemistry
between you could heat

                  a skillet all set to sizzle or wait while you separate
                          an onion into hemispheres of cool
could slice this crisp
icy globe could break

                    something in the house fills with tears in the eyes
                  prism the root into glassy chips whose attraction to
butter softens
them into little windows each with its own

                              clarified view of the cleaver
                      and the chopping block off enough time
for the wild
rice to absorb the subtle

                    tones of wine and sea salted broth could season
                      this friable landscape of spice curry flavor
to set florets and cubes
aglow in evening lime light in the coconut milk melting

               candle wax snow small green marjoram patches of ground
                   pepper the conversation with gesturing forks
over the moon spooning
up such a gourmet meal you could cook up a feast

                          out of the deep freeze could keep
                            fresh meat from going bad

House of Clothing

Because the house is another garment   attached but separate the darks

and lights the way you should   be with each other the house can relate

to the clothes hung up   about the closet the drying rack

you spread with shed layers   mood changes indecision first impressions

turned inside out into a more wrinkled   desire for the former life

and movement of your own bodies   forms give them an escape a game

to play with hemming raw edges and closure gone 3D the house wonders if

you think you are what you are made of or what you make of that   or what

you take off last whether   you are alone or you are not your clothes

are bandages over your shame   on you a shell a shield a wash

rinse spin together container and contained   reveal or conceal yourself you

should still cover   for one another

and your own identity   crisis with a citrus scent betrayed by doppelgängers

can't mask the dampening of night   sweats and underthings get intimate

in the laundry basket nestling between your pants   and your pants press bare skin to bare skin through the cycles   slough off all but the necessities

the essence of you and your clothes hamper yourselves in order to sort it all

out the unclean   from the clean

Dust

The house is interested in the flow patterns   of dust
wonders what are dust's contents

part skin part wall   a melding of all
intimate   triangulating

forms   of dormant comets eclipse the carpets
under coffee tables meanders swirl their dry froth up

from subterranean riverbeds   ellipses and vortices
of air from shuffling feet whirlpool and spiral

hair pollen ash into ghosts   souvenirs
for a memoirist with a microscope

extended meditations on the relative angles   of sunbeams and floors
the house believes

dust is alive a quiet but not shy tenant   shadow of itself
fiber   fleck and flake

in need of coddling   envies its tiny indignant
tornadoes its horizontal stalagmites

navigating corners its subversive movements   through corridors
of lint

eyelash   crumb
seed   of an idea beneath a chair grown roots

visible in cahoots
knits

a wake in reverse
with death dust's

phantom limb
the path dust follows

what about the broom
and reconfigures

the artist's brush

the broom draws
and unfurls again

Mice

The house is of time not space age comes in time

                                   for death all along is a shadow
of itself lately longing for analysis

                                   of heights and breadths and R-values
of thirty or more so you pawn then for now phase

                                   out the old and in the new
idea of you as if as you revise you could

                                                        freeze
time no sooner is every hinge and strip of trim driven in

                                   to place than you start a new tack
on an addition take out a wall

                                   while mouse by mouse hollows
nests in gnawed fiberglass anymore you never

                                   get warm even turning up the thermostat to heat
the entire state of New Hampshire

                                   turning over under covers
cells replacing mimetic cells every seven years

                                   itch in places mice come and go but you can't
reach or measure when change became

                                   change what point it was too late
for a house to ever be perfect

                                   but maybe you still could be
upgrading the windows and storms reframing

                                   cold drafts of who you are collecting
like kibble inside winter boots you put your foot in fall

                                   caches of seeds hidden behind spice jars
you out of another renovation plan

                                   your next move like so many
pieces of furniture you take

                                   for granted how many

versions of you there are two by two

                                        by four you don't know

if you would choose a skyscraper loft or the country château today

                                    over yesterday which is

the real you say you want to be

                             yourself which one wonders the house

is confused about what you do or don't

                                 repair when you're a little worse

for where did you go

                             through this before like screws newly

working their way back out of the Sheetrock

                        one by one mice eating away all the insulation

The Riven House

Even the floorboards so dry

                                        draw back

from each other for that ironic view so long now

                                they shrink into themselves leaving

gaps like slow digs

                                to China surrounded by gradual cliffs

tipped like the great and natural

                        geographic forms splinter first with a single blade

of fake hay from a storebought broom you flick

                                grains of sand and toast to the surface

vacuum distilled matter till

                                the soil of geologic splits breeds a need

for a spoon to lift

                                evolutionary flint the dust of domestic realms

gone environmentally unstable

                                upheavals raise mountains out of molehills

chasms part for water falls down precipitous

                                stone into arroyos where coyotes bay

at fluorescent moons

                                where you could pose to take another shot

of this grand canyon landscape and send

                                it home with uncharacteristic interest

you reach scraping against scree your hand down fissures

                        past the inner laval place of quaking the board

just to feel

                        in the cooled stream of things the golden carp

nudge what you can't catch

                                voices lilting upward from the buried

silt down there the scent

                        of brewed herbs ceremonial fires leaves

42

an aftertaste a faint

                glow from below at night tints the house

as if from far cities lights

                        obscure the stars

The Recurrent House

Where are you
                                    when you exit and enter through your strange
invisibility like a ghost on the couch
                                    beside you the shadow of another
time goes in search of a change
                                    of walls without scare tactics like
do not listen at the keyholes never open
                                    this third room hypnotized by the mystery
of a distant
                                    whirring of wheels repeating clinks of glass
and ice a threatening hum
                                    like the falling hush of hair
behind a heavy door wandering you reconsider
                                    the option to disobey the thrill of the unforeseen
consequences till you're lost in the circular
                                    stairwells in every corner overlaps up
with down and east with west a missed guess an emptiness
    at the center where there should be shouldn't there be an inner chamber
or at least a great hall you're afraid or are you
                                                            hoping
you might fall
                                                            over the threshold thorns
on ancient roses below a sky
                                    reminiscent of suspension
bridges between recurrent dreams of endless
                                    corridors and turns over
and over you slip between shifting surfaces edge sure
                                    you've been here before but where
you thought you knew the place
                                    of every armoire and chair every bedpost bare

spaces long scratches mar the parquet or
                              unexpected frames scrape your shins
again and again you could swear you hear
                        latches click the click of latches catching no one
answers when you call out no
                                          voice calls from you curl
your hand over the knob believe
                                                      you feel held
gripping of someone
                                          else's on the other side

House of Habit

Who expects the thousandth overheard

                                            whisper to blow into breezes

slam the doors and violate

                                        the habitual order of papers foresees

how it spins into force a hurricane shakes

                                            loose the length and depth

of solid inner workings

                                        clatter like skeletons in their closets

dishes tip

                                            from their shelves

crash

                                                and then

                    in the quiet aftermath of this small personal disaster a single
ray of light sliced a line too bright to face a divide

                                            down the center of the house

is a shift in the winded leaves

                                        a fallen branch between the house

and the sun some swift

                                    repercussion hitting a dead end or turning

a corner maybe a prod

                                        against the season's usual angles

an unexpected equinox a sharper tilt

                                        in the axis at the core who knows who

is to blame for a heated knife cuts

                                    to the quick like an instinct for dwelling

on dread the seduction

                                        of that thin voice in the ear saying

turn away light of joy you

                                            cut away so many times

you don't recognize the blade

                                                you have become

Eyes

House of eyes of rope of slow suicides   and the wind in the trees shadows
the lifeless window   makes moonlight pulse

against walls shudder   through rooms in silence so
twined you can hear the lashes   sweep the pillow with every blink

Time

If   in the house
as the clock chimes   one
two   many
you get claustrophobic remember   when you were another immigrant
refugee without a prayer   who nailed an empty mezuzah beside the door
when you said by this forever   *you live here you kiss*
the carved cup   *of this tiny mailbox*
of God   receives and sends blessings aslant
as the reverberant hours by now   by then before and afterward to want
another house or no other house   is
to wish to abandon the house   is
to   fantasize
death   seals your fate inside one frame
of reference to another life no one leaves   home there is no one who does
not   in time
live here inside no   place that is not the house to go
homeless soul at the stroke of midnight listen   think
you   cannot leave
the house   broken

The Glass House

When daylight breaks and enters cracks
open a window with the sheer force of news the house defines
the difference between what is fragile and what transparent
to the light of day fills you with the more
sustainable substitute for electricity even when it's overcast
this radiant stuff undercuts
your sleep so you wake up to see your way clear to knowing
you've seen through you room by room each room a shard
that pins you down pierces with the question if you could choose
a house of cards a sand castle in the air or the one
that crumbles with a huff and a puff a snow globe blown
of molten glass at the end of a pipe dream house which could possibly
outlast the one you made the one that reflects you
and the other question what are you afraid of
seeing or being seen if you live in a glass house
hang a curtain or two for when the neighbors walk their dogs
or when the moon appears too blunt
a contrast to the sharper sun or this one what kind of blind
is night at night is the sky less present
able to bare eyes or more of a piece with windows
mocking your every move it is not
in the nature of the house to obscure
when even in the dark constancy is a fact
you take for granted you might even be overlooking
your own translucence you flicker reflexive as fireflies
at the eaves glow and fade

like a pair of dimmer switched lamps
your sighs plain as day could break
a chain of lies could be why
through walls looking
of something

shatter so easily
a less stout heart could start
you stare
for the light
more

Walls

Go ahead expose the beams
                                    try the open concept subdued by love seats
islands and throw rugs but please
                    don't complain about the walls each Sheetrocked one once
plastered by a different hand in a different subtle
                                            design stripe swirl half moon wave
hello to each fingerprint of someone like you
                                    have these slogans tear down the walls
don't put up walls that offend the house wants you to know
                                            you misunderstand walls
are boundaries everyone needs
                                    some civilizing factor some structure
to hide behind to hold up
                    the stories and the roof have a little backbone
i.e. a wall
                                            has windows and doors
maybe you should talk more about doors
                    deceptive ones like pocket doors submissive folding doors
fussy latches defensive locks and nervous keys what about knobs
                                    let's talk about knobs not walls
because who controls you not the walls
                                    identify and organize yours from yours
inside from outside in here over there compartmentalize like parts
                    of your brains areas where to be together
or not are natural options to balance
                    individual taste in framing and paint colors places for your things
thrown or dropped yours hung or shelved we all
                            feel a little vulnerable sometimes need
a little personal space and boundaries
                            are not endings but definitions to rest within

lean against pass through
                    remember those knobs retreat back through
now houselings square up
                      this wall between you and the walls
with how you love suspense a tease a glimpse
             around a corner the angles you step into and out of
shadow and light hour by hour freed through doorways
                  waiting or moving down the halls
you know those times when you sit in a room
             and it's nice the house tucked around you
like a vow how could you
                        without walls

House of Birds

One winter day a bird flies into the house when it was only air
                                     you wanted and what was it that the bird

wanted the wild viney passion
                          flower never flowers in here it makes itself

at home you have four safe walls and you can't wait
                             to leave to flower elsewhere then you don't

you just want their limits the bird
                          finds the doorway you open for it is gone and then

as if everything else flourishes attracts
                                 its opposite turns inside out two birds

through the smallest opening you left now
                             are in the house you don't even see how

they can fly so fast in so narrow
                          an option they take no time to home in on

every potted out of place plant trancing on its tropical roots
                          volcanoes rain forests heat and beaches reaching

over oceans toward these double glazed windows in turn leaning against
                                                    zero degrees

of separation between seasons spring limb
                    from limb will rise as if death were not so much a boundary

as a border someone you know you are a pattern
                    of contrary habit a patter of wings at both sides of a door

closing
                              what is the opposite of two birds in the house

the opposite
                                                                    of love

House in the Garden

While the house stays true

to its foundation ivy and wisteria take leave

of their trellises and wall

the clapboards even from here it's plain to see

the weeds and garden walk

the lupine skip

down toward the road every year

flirtily glance over a shoulder

farther and farther along equally aloof

lilies of the valley indifferent ferns the flighty daisies evening

primrose negotiate and stake

new boundaries reshape

the grounds like you rearranging

furniture so unreliable

to never stay put never settle

for one color one form to never be tamed or still

you go on sowing seeds love

the garden and trees even the heavy trees

walk away to the distant field

day after day

the house can't

help

cringing as vines creep up new heights cling

to shingles with crawling reach

this rose that rose thorn thorn another thorn in the siding why

do you touch them stand

their noxious cuttings upright in pretty pitchers

clasp

those pithy sticks with their little

tensile clips their endless trips

up drainpipes down steps the house
                              has stood in the yard where the first stems
to grow the first flowers rained
                              into soil clean of clay and stone prone
to the slightest wind or passing wasp
                              fade and dry brown and die back and yet
come to life over and over there and there far
                                        far from their first roots

like some series of fickle
                                        reincarnation

affairs and you are taken
                                        in as if

the house in staying here
                              stunted your bloom

The Disappearing House

Because the curve of the wood as it grew up in the forest unbalances
                              the house mimics the catena of the world needs
a spirit level and aplomb unfound the house
                                             dreams of falling
and falling and does not wake up
                        before hitting the ground tears the intricate understory
of living things the exoskeletons of grave diggers
            sunders the potsherds of past civilizations displaces worms between
fractures of stone beneath stone strips rivulets and obstructs
                                    openings too dark to call open
the house can't stop falling goes on
                        below as above the organ of siding remains
intimate with everything like your skin a porous border
                              pummeled by elements and touch
where you begin
                              to tell the difference between splinters
of moonlight and glass and wood and rock
                                    sparking outward from the shattered
loam of eons of deserts of seas of wildernesses of cities the ancestors
            of horses and wrens and trees and feathers and skulls the petrified
glorious goings on of the dead
                                          still falling
in love with the other
                              side of your affinities the infinite
weather you are never not
                              falling on and on and never
not a dream still sinking into the earth till the more
 soiled the more time tunneled and buried the more embedded here you are
the more you
                                    disappear

The Living Room

When finally you turn out the lights and go to bed

the house stays up late into the night

opens

out

in

peace stretches out

on the recliner across the couch a soft patch

of light quiet on cushions

the bright padded

moon shows through a blanket

of clouds the sky takes

shape now infinity figures

in framed squares glows through wherever is

not wall is glass

window wall

window

wall sky wall

infinity

house

alternate like your breaths

taken in and let go

back to bed now this time is the house's

outlet sighs with relief

to be left unplugged switchplates off not needing to recede

from groping hands

molding and baseboards nestle in

to the Sheetrock

here

and there

on endtables books close their mouths over secrets

the house sees you keep

                                          waking hopes you stay in bed under the covers let
the sofa stuffing expand around its contrast

                                          piping released from the weight of your naked
dissatisfactions restlessly shifting from your thoughts

                                                    to your body
thought

                                                        body
asleep

                                                    awake
your own wall

                                          against the windows
natural midnight lightly

                                              vibrating inside
and out

                                          like the piano's strings
attached to what stays alive

                                                overnight
the rest

                                                needed
to soothe the hinged doors of cupboards creak

                                      still the iron knobs loosened in the wood
cooling in the stove grayblack in the infinite

                                                dark
mortar and bricks escape

                                            the house
through the chimney smoke rises freely

                                                first
lingering in the air above the roof

                                              a last
glance back

The Bedroom

Isn't it enough more than enough for you simply to live in the house simply
to be   awake in it to it again this morning to know it
exists around you newly sprung with light or rain   you know the house
watches over you   more than enough
that you never have to knock to be let in   for you are all
the doors to the house   admits you and just enough
of the sound of wind   chimes in the eaves outside your bedroom
soothe you   made your bed and laid in it lifted the covers
slid your legs linked in the fresh expanse of clean   percale beside yourself
every corner and alcove   yields without a reason
to importune   you know the answer
is yes   make up
your minds you do not need any more   to sleep
on it   is enough

House Cleaning

You know sometimes the house feels   like a dump for instance maybe
before you go away or when you come back   you could pay

a little attention to detail act like you care to notice where the cobwebs dull
the plaster how much dust   dims the shelves because did you

know that neglected houses deteriorate faster than tended ones   so once
in a while will you clear the air stop overlooking dead bulbs in lamps needs

to take out the trash make good   a promise to scrub and to sweep
under your bed and bureau at least occasionally   get down on your knees

with a rag a sponge around the grimed toilet rim drag out   the vac plump
the pillows feel for   what's lurking there leaking pens sticky nickels dimes

loose change isn't the same   as tidiness still when was the last time
you touched the house this way   unhurried a little possessive

about where things go what belongs   there there is a place
for everything too much to ask all right   enough you already wiped that

down you could rub it raw   scratch the finish push
the furniture too far from its dark indents   otherwise next to godliness

the house wants to be neatly   accepted for what is or at least what you
ought to know could be by now   and then either you work with

what you've got   alongside each other like parallel lines
said to meet somewhere or else you know a place   could get too perfect

you're like a Venn diagram all codependent overlap   how about
you compromise with good enough for that comfortably lived in look a spot

less reputation wasn't   what the house had in mind
and won't let anyone feel   at home

The Bathroom

For one Amazonian moment in the house's rainy season you peel
                              off your clothes sigh to be free and then
naked and exposed there
                              is a rustling behind the shower curtain some swung
monkey coiled to the vine and peeking
                              around the pulled plastic freshly splashed
with tiny tears caught in the lashes of a tribe
                              indignant at your mission
of a single moment of privacy must be
                              mocked monkey by monkey with little fists
clutching the towel hooks your futile dream of solitude
                              to a fevered desire to mimic a desert
ambience with the tiles' hard reds the room's dry ochres out in the open
                              spaces one spies under the clouds
of condensation another
                              hungry one drumming
up and down on the washing machine
                              two under the overturned basket
of soiled laundry more rolling
      across the linoleum toilet paper ribbons root in the ceiling fans whoop
at their good fortune to be here now
                              in your bathroom
you steam and whirl
                              and listen through the singing stream
from the shower head for the baby
            oil slicks the floor more sticky clinging fingers flinging a coconut
cream rinse crying across the canopy more sliding the mango soap
                  just beyond sight unblinking barking your skin crawling
in the tropical humidity of jungle leaves traces
                              large as washcloths and deep

as the woven mulch of bath mats your hair
                              tangled with their rubbery clamping handlike
paws screech wiping clear the mirror
                              to find your face your breasts seen not
only seen but needed and judged
                              by a jury of your peering
monkeys scratching and picking
                              everywhere they can with their long curling
arms reach your body at last a tree
                              to be climbed to all that is ripened
good
                                                                  fruit

to be mouthed and chewed

House of Cards

House of the axis and the ax the *x*   and the *y* human and hewn
in spades you can pick   apart the crossing vertical and horizontal
ribbons open the house like a gift   or a tomb but the house
an overturned card   remains
a mystery the how and the why   of it an act of faith a lyric
and is that the problem   or the point the what the
or the is   to visit or to live
from the heart dependent on how steady the hand dealt you want the house
to stand   for something some physical manifestation of
marriage or meaning an avatar   prophet or prophecy
you also love reason being   what you make of it
with sleight of hand two of one kind of another   balanced on edges
stretching from floor to ceiling   the full house may be your keeper
your strength your stronghold   or your strangler
a club that would have you   as its dues paying member
if not for the precarious how   could the diamond hard fate
refract such light   you can't look
straight at it till it all comes tumbling down your poker face   the stories
of the whole construction project fluttering   free

Furniture

The better to peer over your decor here
                                    is a braided red rope with brass hooks
to a supporting wall partially removed
                                                    from the heart
of the house's threshold
                                            of change and rearrange
mean haltings in the hallway scarred with scuff marks
                                    the trail of a heavy desk where you wrote
off any former scribbler who took a turn
                                    to recline against your armchair wings
angled just so
                                    as to hide the archaeological strata
of multiple reupholsterings visible through tears
                                            in your crocheted coverlets
your memory become a curtain thin
                                    as the veneer on two farflung families'
furnishings marrying hutch to trunk to bed frame to dish
                                    on interior designs of your own
reflections in heirloom silver and lamp shades the eternally
                                    borrowed bureaus brown from use
after use make use
                                    of overlapping legacies splinter the estates
hopes and heresies of museum quality
                                            regrets wear the finish the story
of furniture is the story of the mortal
                                    coil unraveling *le réveil mortel*
resurrecting story upon story into one house divided
                                            against itself cannot stand
to lose even a single piece removes each
                                            life living in its own

lifetime all lifetimes at once
                                  upon a time becomes an order in the generations
of fingerprints you share an emigration
                                           of ownership and lives dovetail
the mortise and tenon of negative space relations
                                      you negotiate between the shapes of things

The Junk Drawer

The house admits it doesn't like the junk drawer
                                    its pretense of importance like the narcissist's
casual affect its mindlike reserves of absurdity
                                            access the past and the house
is afraid of the past with its secreted shames and dreams you can hide there
                                                    old lives old loves
among the single edge razor blades bells and plastic black spiders creep
    out the house not so much when you shuffle picture hooks and stiffened
rubber bands or claw farther back
                        to empty penny rolls loose pennies unblown birthday balloons
condensed and cramped to make room
                        for newer gluesticks and twist ties but when you mindlessly
manifest the most inaccessible
                                            stores of the drawer is an unedited diary
an elevated irrelevance of object and deny you keep
            doohickies sad as dry moist towelettes or eyeglasses without arms
chipped little teardrops for holding a mirror up to a wall
        in this drawer the past is naked as a button and as hopeful for closure
but how unimpoverishable you must think you are
                                            with a drawer like that
could prepare you for anything any sudden need
                            to sprinkle air through a jarless punctured lid
to roll the single die to live it all again to leave it to chance encounter
                        the present memory of the wine tilted celebration
from which you saved this cork gone past
            but at least you have the cork is something who knows which thing
will catch you off guard and take you
                            away from the house wonders if you save to be free
to forget or forget because you save
                            each thing you hold onto simply

because it was there it was yours but the house doubts that you should
                                        take prisoners hostage
now to then squirrel the hostile world of things
                        combined to rubble rumbling in its sliding tracked
wooden box way to never
                        make up your mind whether it serves or subtracts
to save the past as if from oblivion a waste
                                        land of the lost
thingamabobs paraphernalia of the parenthetical you hope you are not
                        yet the house has seen it all every defunct
appointment card pocket guide to your chakra
                energy centers tweezer and clothespin and tomorrow will shift
six unsharpened monogrammed souvenir
                pencils perpendicular to the drawer and jam it shut for good

Arson

You don't know jack

                built this house around your volatile pain refers
to yourself in the third person periodically flares up

                     without a functional fire

extinguisher there is no pronoun

                         for the house is

your illusion an illness

                    that doesn't let you feel

settled despite

             how you choose to believe you can be
in the house every time you burn

          it down in your arsenic rages hot then cool
down gather up from the toxic ashes

                   the nails you need
to raise the next house around the same

                    unstable mood

disorder demanding what

         is the drill where in hell is the hammer saw
in two every inch you are

            not separate from the house is your

false construct

               for not one single second
person plural defines a relationship or a name for what you keep doing

              to you everything is
a home improvement dream project deferred

          eternally not finishing parts you never

notice what you neglect

                    to trim out the cellar smoldering again

off gassing off limits the spontaneous

             combustion rags the rusting boiler pipes inflated

tires spinning by the explosive blown

                  fuses spark your flinty temper

is not a viable address your indoor life

                      in your indoor voice

will you

                    file the insurance claims

you null and void

                  by reason of insanity your face

in the mug shots inflamed

Hoarding

The house unlike you loves the passage
                                        of time archipelagoes
times treasured and revised while you knit a bridge
                            your rooms with old news cards receipts
certificates planners and periodicals those islandish
                                        documents spin
a single landmass for you crawl from corners down the hall
                        and up staircases scribing ceilings and attic hatches
the subjective world a planet in detail sticking to its own ecosystem
                                        with a street address lest
you forget how you arrived and where before disintegrating
                            like the sediments that made of Troy
nine Troys less revisionist histories
                    told on tablets and tearable as the wings of houseflies
than the wine talking sentimentally and then the thud
                            of cosmic rock crashed to unearth
in increments the very thing you meant to save destroying
                        what you meant to save each spoke of the wheel of
life lost in collecting records to counter loss
                                    looms when you throw away
moment after moment in vain refusal
                        to lose a moment passing as you cry for the others passed
are buried in paper piers
                                        throughout the house
thinks you could be more
                                        like the spider
overnight constructs a web so thick
                        it sounds like parchment wrapping and unwrapping
each day no matter how many times you crumble it
                            always weaves another home

The Real House

If you believe you are   in
a house then the house is real on its own terms   of endearment to yourself
begetting yourself in a frame   work of a nest made
manifest in the magic   act
of home dec or a domestic chore that enlightens   your load
of chopped wood and carried water   fills the space
and time allotted you   might if you could
believe you will die   when you die
you will leave   the house
will leave   you so much room
to live without a footprint   so vast it's visible from a star
is   a star
so radiant   you
might believe you are too much   the universe
too great   a leap
a bird   who can fly
if the bird   believes it is
flying who   falls

House Warming

This house out of the wind   is a little nirvana lit
by the million and one time   to have been alive in it chosen it come home
to it built of the found and scrounged   the considered and created
shapes of your lives   in the house wants you to understand
you never disappoint when you don't love what the house loves but you do
from the bottom of your   feet as they glide on the floor as the floor
supports you never anymore have to be   wary prey here you know whereof
each creak speaks a language   you learned without learning how to say
welcome welcome in every direction   is a weathervane in a warm spell
ing all the news you need to take   sometimes a day
to sweep the walls to bow   a soft cloth in your hand to every surface
reminds you of you without trying to the house   presses its palm back
day after day is a diary you confide in   telling page after page to save
your life for another chance to be born   under cover of this single
ceiling you are   a child attuned as a fed predator hiding
under your parents' bed under rumpled sheets   pillows stained
from baby teeth anchor   your losses to silver coins always find
a way to you   like the welcome sounds now of snow
melting off shingles   glittering in the February thaw where the private
underpinnings of bed boughs and springs can uphold   the inconceivable
origins of you and the air   compresses between dust ruffles
the secret flint of your skin   and bones in the room the parting beads
of the windows catch every breath you've ever breathed   through curtains
a valentine   of setting sun
lengthens afternoon even as your days   grow shorter come down at last
to one   long sigh of the roof above you freeing from the ice

The Porch

The house is one rent heaven divisible by rooms
partition stellar spaces between sticks

close to the hearth
true the house is an introvert

domestic deriving
strength from the inner life needs

too a henge the fringe
a partially attached partner not un

reconciled to a lack of thermostats all wind
and whim under shelter

of the great outdoors with a floor on a porch
is a sabbath a pause never wasted

time out of time with the blue
buttoned up roof leaning back

against the open end outside
wall of the house facing the start of something

else some greater inside
information on garden street passerby bridge and sky and all

the foreign and wide other

walls of train stations shops and concert halls factories and temples
aspiring briefly
between infinite distances

circle back to the front
door beyond construct

or happenstance the porch part solid part air
with your lips

for sound
and sense of the substantial

conversation of joists and purlins with the strata of cloud
audible here in the particulate smattering of one small safe

house party
to the world at large

House of Pie

One July's preverbal dawn when you are still in bed you drift
                                      into the kitchen on bare feet can only think

in images your mind's a baby's
                                      picturebook in which you read

apple you read *countertop* and *cup* smile at *water*
            stretching inside its *teapot* a still cool wind feathers the flames shear

like heated honey on the tongue
            beyond the screen's the tick like a timer a seed a second in the beaks

of nuthatches and house finches at the feeder beginning
                                      to wake up you picture *song in the throat*

think yellow green dream of a breakfast of egg and onion and pear
                                      for two pillowed

in turmeric marjoram remember last night
                                      how you savored the sighs of *you* stirring

asleep in the sheets
                        the sweetness of *your hair* you didn't know you touched

with your mouth turn back another page read evening *dusk*
            rafters coated with smoke from pie filling overflowed

till it glazed the oven floor with blueberry
                        bruised teeth you tasted yesterday between times you spoke

aloud although quietly through *the open skylights*
                                      the house went on breathing for you

as you reached your *spoon across the table*
                                      and dipped it into the other dish *your dish*

House of Rain

As if the wind ascends stirred
              by leaves and not the other way around the house you can hear
from your comforter first leaf another leaf after leaf every leaf
                              ticking down branch by branch
what it must be like
                     to be a living tree the house has no memory
of timber mills its own songs
               in fallen canopies its own snows dusting down
surfaces spring free and when rain comes now it is only rain
                here and nowhere else for no one else knows
weather anywhere but here there
                  is rain or no rain only maybe paths taken
by soaked leaves falling
               to the rain layers you and you weight drop
upon drop plaiting into deltas spread small maps
                   of years accumulate on glass
ballast the house floats tiny acorns on the sky lights
               up rain slipping into what buckets can't hold
buckling and disheveling till there is nothing
            to be done nothing not undone but the wind wanting nothing
but to come in
                  warm to meet your skin halfway
open windows in love with air flow drunk
                   on rain the selvedges pine
and oak sills rise from year to year life to life
             echoes lumber seasons of slumber and sun
lift apart planed rings like spools of thread
           time unwinds you at last drink to you in the storm
through every room drinking what you can
             carry rain in your hands imperfect cups

House of Happiness

Sometimes you think that happiness is a very   thin veil fragile as the body

it envelops and you think   that happiness is not

what you want to wear   or you think happiness is a

house promising as the marriage   it shelters

and you think that happiness   is not

where you want to live   but what you are

The Word for House

Begin with the word for the long spine extending

                    one double door against which for closure

the other comes to rest

                        when there are no longer

words for *other* or for *door* begin

                  while your tea brews and cools to wait

for heaven

                            knows what

song the spirit sings or where

                      it begins like the sky clearing up

secrets never told until

                      everyone knows nothing

that begins

                          or ends is God

a household name your final prayer or the first

                      word canceling all need

for further needs explanations for the carpets

                  unattached to floors the hours ticking away

from the clocks water poured forth free of faucets

                  the astragal stripped loose from the door

has no name

                    lifting to the stars like wings spilling

all words for elsewhere beginning once

                there was a cup of tea or two one day a house without

time

                    to swallow or confide what you meant

to say unhinged it hits you

                      could live here forever

if forever

                    were a word for something

that forever could be called that if

                you could begin to love enough you could

begin to be

                          unhoused

Acknowledgments

A Cappella Zoo, Spring 2012,"The Bathroom"

Adanna, Summer 2011, "House in the Garden"

Alice Blue Review, 2014: "The Recurrent House," "House of Arson"

Amoskeag, Spring 2013, "Hoarding," "The Living Room"

Construction, August 2012, "The Doubtful House," "The Glass House"

Crazyhorse, Fall/December 2011, "House of Habit"

Cross Review, 2015, "House Charges"

Green Mountains Review "The Housing"

Hotel Amerika, Fall 2011; appeared Jan. 2012, "House of Talk," "Thieves," "The Word for House"

Inflectionist Review, Summer 2013, "House of Happiness" (Pushcart & Best of Web Nominee)

Massachusetts Review, 2013, "Footfalls"

Mom Egg Review, 2015, "The Bedroom"

Rat's Ass Review, 2016, "House Keys"

No Tell Motel, September 2011, "House of Clothing," "House Cleaning," "House of Answers," "House of Rain," "Anniversaries"

Ozone Park, Fall/December 2011, "The Kitchen"

Spillway, Tebot Bach Press, "House of Birds" (December 2011) "House of Cards" (Summer 2012)

Spittoon, December 2013, "The Riven House," "Playhouse," "The Closet"

Talisman: A Journal of Contemporary Poetry & Poetics, 2014, "House of Mirrors," "Dust,"* "House of Time," "Walls," "The Real House," "House Warming"

*"Dust" also appears as a broadside from the *Worcester County Poetry Association, MA*